Earthquakes

By Jack Zayarny

www.av2books.com

MEDIA ENHANCED BOOKS
AV2 BY WEIGL™
ADDED VALUE · AUDIO VISUAL

AV[2] provides enriched content that supplements and complements this book. Weigl's AV[2] books strive to create inspired learning and engage young minds in a total learning experience.

Your AV[2] Media Enhanced books come alive with...

Audio
Listen to sections of the book read aloud.

Key Words
Study vocabulary, and complete a matching word activity.

Go to **www.av2books.com**, and enter this book's unique code.

Video
Watch informative video clips.

Quizzes
Test your knowledge.

BOOK CODE

Y760898

Embedded Weblinks
Gain additional information for research.

Slide Show
View images and captions, and prepare a presentation.

AV[2] by Weigl brings you media enhanced books that support active learning.

Try This!
Complete activities and hands-on experiments.

... and much, much more!

Published by AV[2] by Weigl
350 5th Avenue, 59th Floor
New York, NY 10118
Websites: www.av2books.com   www.weigl.com

Library of Congress Control Number: 2014934853
ISBN 978-1-4896-1202-1 (hardcover)
ISBN 978-1-4896-1203-8 (softcover)
ISBN 978-1-4896-1204-5 (single-user eBook)
ISBN 978-1-4896-1205-2 (multi-user eBook)

Printed in the United States of America in North Mankato, Minnesota
1 2 3 4 5 6 7 8 9 0 18 17 16 15 14

052014
WEP090514

Senior Editor: Aaron Carr
Art Director: Terry Paulhus

Every reasonable effort has been made to trace ownership and to obtain permission to reprint copyright material. The publishers would be pleased to have any errors or omissions brought to their attention so that they may be corrected in subsequent printings.

Photo Credits
Weigl acknowledges Getty Images as its primary photo supplier for this title.

Contents

Earthquakes are One of the Deadliest Natural Disasters in the World

Earthquakes are sudden shifts in the layers the make up Earth. Earth has four main layers. These layers are the inner core, outer core, mantle, and crust. The outer part of the planet is made of the crust and the top of the mantle. This outer part is made up of many separate pieces that are always in motion. These pieces are called tectonic plates. They can be thousands of miles (kilometers) in length. These plates often slide and bump into each other. Earthquakes happen when tectonic plates move and come in contact with each other.

Some places, such as Japan and the west coast of the United States, are located near or on the seams where two tectonic plates meet. This is why these places have more earthquakes than others. Earthquakes cause about 10,000 deaths worldwide each year. Until recently, it was thought that all earthquakes were caused by natural processes. However, scientists have found that humans can cause earthquakes as well. Digging, oil drilling, building dams, and other industrial activities can trigger tectonic shifts that can cause earthquakes.

Cleaning up the damage caused by earthquakes can take months of work.

On March 11, 2011, one of the most powerful earthquakes ever recorded caused widespread damage in Japan.

Most Earthquakes are Caused by Geological Faults

Most earthquakes happen along **fault lines**. These are areas where two tectonic plates brush, pull, or push against one another. There are four different types of faults. The types are based on the direction in which the tectonic plates move.

TYPES OF GEOLOGICAL FAULTS

NORMAL FAULT	REVERSE FAULT	THRUST FAULT	STRIKE-SLIP FAULT
This type of fault occurs when two tectonic plates are pulling apart from each other. In a normal fault, the inner block moves down into the space left by the moving plates. The outer blocks along the edges of the plates stay the same height.	This type of fault happens when two tectonic plates push against each other. As the plates put pressure on the fault line, the crust between them is pushed together. A part of the crust moves up and over the ground. In extreme cases, these types of faults can form mountains.	Like a reverse fault, a thrust fault is also the result of two tectonic plates pushing against each other. In a thrust fault, a layer of Earth's crust is pushed over top of another by the force of the impact of the plates. These faults have a layer of older rock sitting on top of a layer of younger rock.	In a strike slip fault, the fracture in the crust caused by the movement of tectonic plates is **vertical**. The pieces of the crust move side to side because of the pressure, unlike the vertical movement in other types of faults.

The edges of tectonic plates sometimes become stuck together over time. As the plates move, pressure builds up along the edges. The movement of the plates eventually forces them to rip away from one another. The surface where this separation takes place is called the fault plane.

When plates separate, the built-up pressure is released. This energy travels in the form of **seismic** waves. These waves travel through the ground, shaking the earth.

The Lavic Lake fault in San Bernardino, California, can be seen as a huge crack in the ground.

Natural Causes
Plates, Volcanoes, and Landslides

10–20 MILES
(16–32 kilometers) is the area that the effects are felt after a volcanic earthquake.

20
The surface of the Earth is covered by 20 plates that are always moving. This movement is what causes most earthquakes.

80%
This is the percentage of all earthquakes that take place deep underwater in the Pacific Ocean.

VS

Human Causes
Mining, Oil Drilling, Nuclear Testing, and Dam Building

Over the past 30 years, the number of earthquakes each year in the United States has risen from 20 to more than 100.

347 MILLION TONS
(315 million metric tons) The weight of water at a huge dam in China is believed to have caused an earthquake in 2008.

DRILLING for oil or other resources has been linked to several earthquakes around the world.

Earthquakes
Cannot be Prevented

A variety of very powerful forces within the Earth cause earthquakes. People cannot usually stop earthquakes from happening. However, it is possible to predict when and where an earthquake will happen. It is also possible to prepare for the earthquake's effects and prevent some of the damage done to buildings and other structures.

There are many ways to detect signs of earthquakes before the earthquakes begin. Some scientists claim that animal behavior can be used as a precursor to predict when and where an earthquake can strike. In some cases, animals are able to sense weak **tremors** or shifting tectonic plates. The animals will then quickly leave the area in large numbers. However, this method of prediction is not reliable, as animals tend to behave differently in different situations.

The top floor of the Transamerica Pyramid building in San Francisco swayed more than 12 inches (30 centimeters) side to side during an earthquake in 1989, but the building was not damaged.

In Japan, where earthquakes are common, **engineers** have created buildings that are "earthquake-proof." One type of building sits on top of an inflatable airbag. When an earthquake is detected, the airbag expands and absorbs the impact of the quake, leaving the building unharmed.

In Japan, schoolchildren are given fire-proof hats to wear in the event of an earthquake.

Other buildings, like the Transamerica Pyramid in San Francisco, use more complex methods to avoid damage. Some buildings use machines called base isolators. These are sets of two parallel horizontal plates. The bottom plate sits on the ground, while the building stands on the top plate. The two plates are attached to each other, but do not move together. When an earthquake hits and the ground shakes, only the bottom plates move back and forth. The top plates "float," with the bottom plates stopping the energy released by the quake from reaching the actual building.

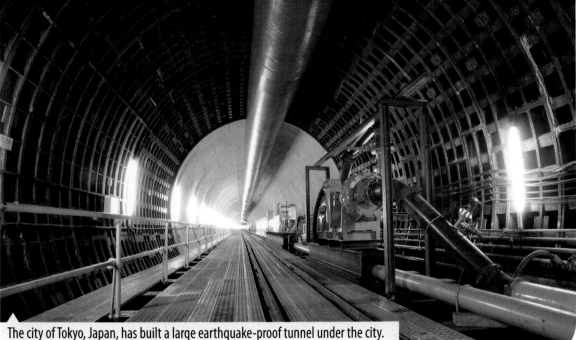
The city of Tokyo, Japan, has built a large earthquake-proof tunnel under the city. The tunnel is meant to protect water pipes and wiring for phones and the internet.

Somewhere on Earth, an Earthquake Occurs every 30 Seconds

Earthquakes happen often throughout the world. On average, there is an earthquake happening every 30 seconds. Almost 500,000 earthquakes happen every year around the world. Most of these earthquakes are too small to be felt. They do very little damage. These earthquakes can only be detected by special tools. Tools can help predict where and when larger earthquakes may take place. About 100,000 earthquakes per year are strong enough to rattle windows and shake houses. In Japan, these types of earthquakes are common. Many people attach furniture to the floor and make their houses stronger with special materials to prevent damage from shaking and moving objects.

Earthquakes that hit major cities can cause billions of dollars in damage.

Only about 100 earthquakes a year cause significant damage and are a danger to human lives. These quakes usually take place in specific areas that are at high risk for tectonic plate activity, such as southern California, Indonesia, Japan, and China. Large earthquakes that result in widespread damage usually happen once a year. Areas where earthquakes happen often build safer structures and educate people who live there about earthquake safety.

The area in the world that has the largest amount of **seismic activity** is known as the Pacific Ring of Fire. This is a horseshoe-shaped region in the Pacific Ocean that has 452 active volcanoes and two of the largest tectonic plates, the Nazca Plate and the Cocos Plate. These plates often push on each other and cause earthquakes. The Ring of Fire is located over the edges of these two plates, where the pressure is highest.

More than 90 percent of the world's earthquakes, and 81 percent of the world's largest earthquakes, take place in the Ring of Fire.

500,000
Number of earthquakes each year around the world.

that is

57 earthquakes each hour

or close to an earthquake every minute.

ONE HUNDRED
Earthquakes cause damage each year.

100,000
The number of earthquakes that can be felt.

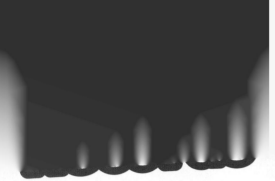

Scientists have kept records of earthquakes since the first quake was recorded in China in 1831 BC. Earthquakes are some of the most damaging natural disasters. Scientists gather data about these events to be able to spot patterns and help protect people and buildings from damage or destruction.

DEADLIEST
The deadliest earthquake ever took place on January 23, 1556, in Shaanxi, China. It caused 830,000 deaths.

STRONGEST
The strongest earthquake ever recorded was in Chile in 1960.

LONGEST

The longest earthquake lasted for 10 minutes. It took place in the Indian Ocean in 2004.

MOST DAMAGING

The 2011 Tōhoku Earthquake in Japan was the most costly earthquake in history. The damage from the earthquake was estimated at $235 billion.

Earthquakes in the United States

There are about 6,000 earthquakes a year in the United States. Most of these quakes happen in coastal areas as a result of tectonic shifts in the ocean. Many are small and do not affect people, but some can be deadly. The strongest earthquakes in the United States take place in Alaska. Most of the other strong quakes take place along the west coast, in California, Nevada, Washington, and Oregon.

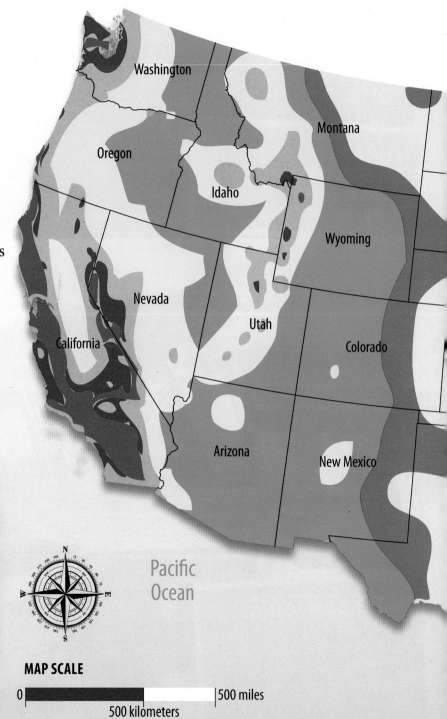

SHAKING (%g)

The unit "g" is acceleration of gravity

HIGH HAZARD
32+
24-32
16-24
8-16
4-8
2-4
0-2
LOW HAZARD

Pacific Ocean

MAP SCALE

0 — 500 miles

500 kilometers

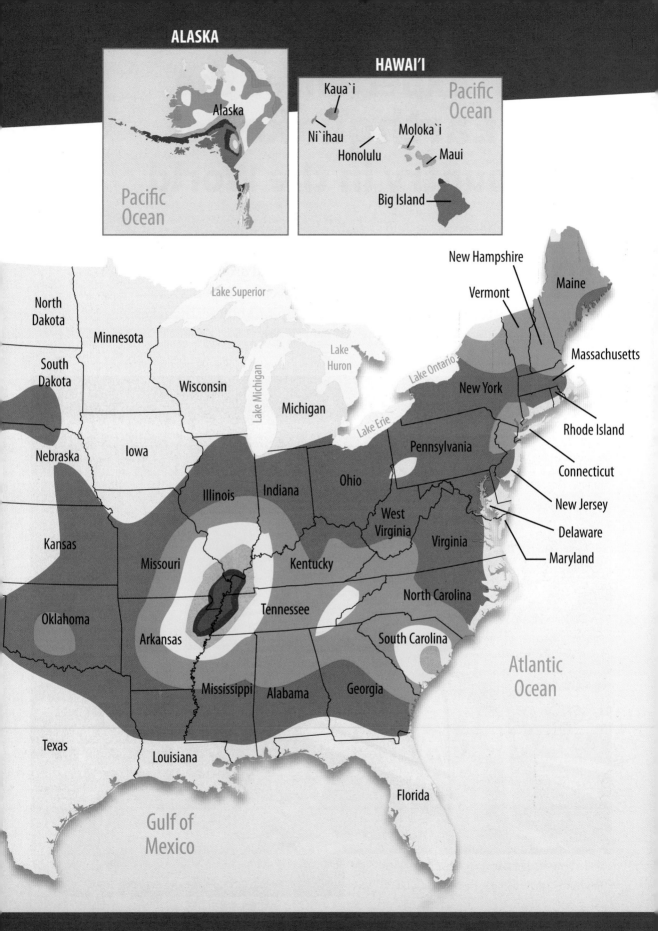

ALASKA

Alaska

Pacific
Ocean

HAWAI'I

Pacific
Ocean

Kaua`i

Ni`ihau

Moloka`i

Honolulu

Maui

Big Island

North
Dakota

Minnesota

Lake Superior

New Hampshire

Maine

Vermont

South
Dakota

Wisconsin

Lake
Huron

Lake Ontario

Massachusetts

Nebraska

Iowa

Lake Michigan

Michigan

Lake Erie

New York

Rhode Island

Pennsylvania

Connecticut

Kansas

Illinois

Indiana

Ohio

New Jersey

West
Virginia

Delaware

Missouri

Kentucky

Virginia

Maryland

Oklahoma

Arkansas

Tennessee

North Carolina

South Carolina

Atlantic
Ocean

Mississippi

Alabama

Georgia

Texas

Louisiana

Florida

Gulf of
Mexico

Japan Experiences the Most Earthquakes of Any Country in the World

Many earthquakes take place in the ocean. About 10 percent of all earthquakes worldwide take place in and around the islands that make up Japan. Small earthquakes, called tremors, can happen as often as every five minutes in Japan. Up to 2,000 earthquakes that can be felt by people happen in Japan every year.

Underwater earthquakes may cause flooding. Often, this leads to more damage than the earthquake itself.

Japan has many earthquakes because it is located at the intersection of four tectonic plates. These plates are the Pacific Plate, North American Plate, Eurasian Plate, and the Philippine Plate. The interaction between these four plates produces many collisions and earthquakes as a result. Japan is also located along one of the edges of the Ring of Fire.

Most of the earthquakes in Japan happen as a result of subduction. Subduction releases a massive amount of energy. In the Ring of Fire, the Pacific Plate is moving at a rate of 3.5 inches (8.9 cm) a year in the direction of the North American Plate. It is being pushed under the North American plate as a result. This causes many of the earthquakes in Japan.

The 2011 earthquake in Japan caused flooding to many parts of Japan's coastline.

1964
Prince William Sound, Alaska

3 minutes
was the length of the strongest earthquake ever to hit the United States

131 people died

$311 million
in property damage, including 30 blocks of downtown Anchorage

An area of 50,000 square miles (130,000 square kilometers) was damaged in the earthquake

American Scientist Charles Richter Invented the Richter Scale in 1935

Most earthquakes around the world are measured using a system called the Richter Scale. The Richter Scale is named after Charles Richter, who created the scale in 1935. The scale gives each earthquake a value based on its strength. The strength of an earthquake is measured by a **seismograph**. According to the Richter Scale, an earthquake that measures a 5.0 will cause shaking that is 10 times stronger than that of an earthquake measuring a 4.0. It will also release 31 times more energy.

The Richter Scale does not have an upper limit. The highest reading on the scale so far has been 9.5, for the Chilean earthquake of 1960. The Richter Scale also does not show the damage done by an earthquake. A weak earthquake can sometimes do more damage than a stronger earthquake.

Charles Richter was an American seismologist and physicist who worked at the California Institute of Technology when he developed the Richter Scale.

The Richter Scale was used to measure earthquakes for more than 30 years. It is currently only used to measure small earthquakes. For large earthquakes, the Moment Magnitude Scale (MMS) is currently used. The MMS was developed in the 1970s. It is more accurate in terms of detecting the amount of energy released by an earthquake. It is also able to provide more details on seismic activity. The MMS is the standard scale used by the **United States Geological Survey (USGS)**. Scales like the MMS are important because they allow **seismologists** to correctly identify the strength of an earthquake and predict whether it will trigger other natural disasters, such as tsunamis. A tsunami is a giant wave that is caused by collisions of the tectonic plates in the ocean. The seismologists are then able to warn governments to evacuate their people from the area. Improvements to both the Richter and Moment Magnitude Scale are being researched by scientists around the world.

Zhang Heng of China invented the first seismometer in AD 132. He used it to detect the direction of an earthquake 310 miles (500 km) away.

John Johnson Shaw was a British scientist who invented the first seismograph to record earthquake activity.

Little Known Facts

TONS OF ENERGY

The energy from a major earthquake is the same as millions of explosives being set off at the same time. A 9.0 earthquake releases the energy of 99 million tons (89 million metric tons) of TNT explosive, or about 25,000 nuclear bombs.

HIDDEN DANGERS

The destruction of buildings and other structures is the main danger during an earthquake. As well, other natural disasters caused by earthquakes, such as tsunamis and landslides, are often more deadly than the earthquakes themselves.

RING OF FIRE

Most of the Earth's seismic and volcanic activity is centered in the Pacific Ocean. The Ring of Fire is an area that is 25,000 miles (40,000 km) long, and is home 75 percent of the world's active volcanoes.

MOVING CITIES

An 8.8 magnitude earthquake in Chile in 2010 moved the city of Concepcion 10 feet (3 meters) to the west. Some seismologists believe that this earthquake also changed Earth's rotation slightly and shortened the length of the day.

ACROSS THE WORLD

Earthquakes on one side of Earth can shake the other side. In 2004, a large earthquake in the Indian Ocean was found to have weakened part of California's San Andreas Fault. Earthquakes can do this by a process called **oscillation**. Oscillation can be measured in scientific stations around the world.

An Earthquake is Strongest at Its Epicenter

The epicenter of an earthquake is the area where the energy of the earthquake is highest. This is where the earthquake is strongest. When scientists identify an earthquake's location, they are usually referring to its epicenter. Earthquakes caused by subduction can have epicenters that are several miles (km) long. These will usually be positioned above the fault line where the tectonic plates moved into or away from each other. The epicenter is directly related to the earthquake's focus. The focus of the quake is where the ground actually breaks as a result of the interaction between tectonic plates.

Earthquakes with a focus of 43.5 miles (70 km) or less do the most damage because the energy is concentrated in a smaller area.

Scientists can try to predict the epicenter of an earthquake by looking at seismograph data. Cities such as Tokyo and Los Angeles are in zones that can have many earthquake epicenters. Scientists need to make a correct prediction to evacuate people if the epicenter is in the middle of a large city. The force of the earthquake can destroy roadways, preventing movement in the city and trapping vehicles and people.

EPICENTER OF AN EARTHQUAKE

Epicenter
The epicenter is the spot on Earth's surface that is above the focus.

Fault scarp
A fault scarp is a steep slope on Earth's surface that results from fault movement.

Fault trace
A fault trace is the line showing the fault on Earth's surface.

Shock waves
Shock waves cause the ground to shake. Some travel inside the Earth while others travel along the surface.

Focus
The focus is the point inside Earth where the earthquake begins.

Fault plane
The fault plane is the place where rock on one side of a fracture has moved in relation to rock on the other side of the fracture.

Earthquakes that Happen Underwater Can Cause Tsunamis

Many countries that are located on islands or near the ocean are at risk for tsunamis. These countries include Japan, Indonesia, and coastal United States. When a large earthquake strikes underwater, the pressure from the collision escapes and pushes large amounts of water to the surface. This water then forms one or more gigantic waves that travel along the surface of the ocean until they hit land.

The total cost of the 2011 Japan earthquake and tsunami disaster was estimated at $235 billion.

Earthquakes below 7.5 on the Richter Scale do not usually cause tsunamis. The fifth largest earthquake in the world since 1900 took place in Japan during 2011. This earthquake measured 8.9 on the Richter Scale and triggered a tsunami that caused damage as far away as California. More than 15,000 people died in the disaster.

OTHER TYPES OF DISASTERS

Tsunami

Tsunami waves can sometimes reach heights of more than 100 feet (30 m) and can travel at speeds of more than 500 miles (805 km) per hour.

Avalanche

Earthquakes in areas with loose snow can cause avalanches. An avalanche is a massive plate of snow that can slide down from a steep slope.

Landslide

A landslide occurs when a layer of soil, mud, and other **debris** shifts down a slope, then becomes more liquid and gains speed. Landslides are often caused by earthquakes and floods. They can be more damaging than the initial event. Every year, landslides in the United States cause $3.5 billion in damage.

In Ancient Greece, People Believed that Poseidon, the Sea God, Caused Earthquakes

Earthquakes have been happening on Earth for as long as the planet has existed. Ancient cultures such as the Greeks and Romans did not have the technology to explain what earthquakes were and how they were caused. They created explanations for these events in the form of **myths**.

The ancient Greeks believed that Poseidon, the god of the seas, created earthquakes when he struck the ground with his **trident** in anger. In India, people believed that the Earth was held up by eight giant elephants. When one of the elephants grew tired, it shook its head, causing an earthquake. A Japanese myth told of a giant catfish that lived under the earth. The catfish was a prankster and could only be controlled by the god Kashima. When Kashima fell asleep, the catfish moved around violently, causing earthquakes.

In addition to the seas, Poseidon was also the god of storms, earthquakes, and horses. He could use his trident to cause a range of disasters, from earthquakes to shipwrecks.

THE STORY OF
POSEIDON

Poseidon was one of the three Greek gods who defeated the **Titans** and gained control over Earth. With his brothers Zeus and Hades, Poseidon chose at random who would control the skies, the waters, and the Underworld. Poseidon chose the waters and was given power over the oceans, seas, and other bodies of water such as lakes and springs.

Poseidon was armed with a large golden trident. He was often called "Earth Shaker", because he had the power to

cause earthquakes. Poseidon could also create powerful sea storms, tsunamis, landslides, and floods. Many of these events were attributed to his wrath when they took place in the ancient world. Offerings of food and riches were given to Poseidon to prevent these disasters.

Only Zeus himself was more powerful than Poseidon. According to legend, Poseidon was not satisfied with his mastery over the seas and challenged Zeus for leadership over the gods. Zeus was stronger, and Poseidon's attempt failed. Despite this, Poseidon kept his power, and many cities in ancient Greece had him as their patron god.

Earthquake Timeline

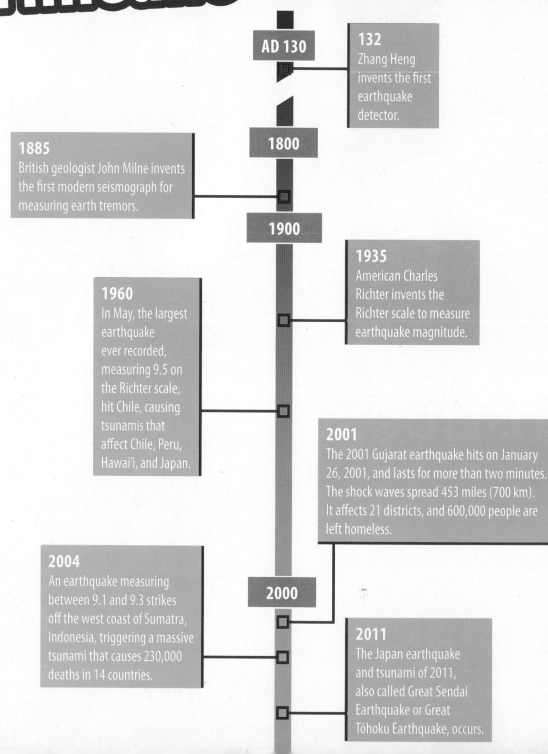

AD 130

132
Zhang Heng invents the first earthquake detector.

1800

1885
British geologist John Milne invents the first modern seismograph for measuring earth tremors.

1900

1935
American Charles Richter invents the Richter scale to measure earthquake magnitude.

1960
In May, the largest earthquake ever recorded, measuring 9.5 on the Richter scale, hit Chile, causing tsunamis that affect Chile, Peru, Hawai'i, and Japan.

2001
The 2001 Gujarat earthquake hits on January 26, 2001, and lasts for more than two minutes. The shock waves spread 453 miles (700 km). It affects 21 districts, and 600,000 people are left homeless.

2004
An earthquake measuring between 9.1 and 9.3 strikes off the west coast of Sumatra, Indonesia, triggering a massive tsunami that causes 230,000 deaths in 14 countries.

2000

2011
The Japan earthquake and tsunami of 2011, also called Great Sendai Earthquake or Great Tōhoku Earthquake, occurs.

Test Your Knowledge

1 How many deaths per year are earthquakes responsible for?

A. About 10,000

2 What is the area between two tectonic plates where most earthquakes happen called?

A. A fault

3 Who invented the first device to detect earthquake activity?

A. Zhang Heng invented the first seismometer in AD 132.

4 How often do earthquakes happen in the world?

A. Every 30 seconds

5 What two largest tectonic plates are present in the Ring of Fire?

A. The Nazca Plate and the Cocos Plate

6 What process causes most of the earthquakes in Japan?

A. The movement of four tectonic plates that intersect beneath Japan

7 What are the two main scales used to measure the strength of earthquakes?

A. The Richter Scale and the Moment Magnitude Scale (MMS)

8 How strong was the most powerful earthquake ever recorded, and where did it take place?

A. A magnitude 9.5 earthquake that hit Chile in 1960

9 Where will most of the damage during an earthquake occur?

A. The epicenter

10 What was the name of the Japanese god who kept watch over the giant catfish under the earth?

A. Kashima

Disasters happen anytime and anywhere. Sadly, when an emergency happens you may not have much time to respond. The Red Cross says that one way to prepare is by assembling an emergency kit. Once disaster hits you will not have time to shop or search for supplies. If you have gathered supplies in advance, you will be prepared.

1 A disaster kit can be for emergency use or can be reusable. Emergency kits are small and have food, water, and medicine. These supplies last only a few days. Reusable kits are larger and can last from a week to a month.

2 Plan the supplies for the kit ahead of time. Choose a package that can be sealed. The package should be tough and easy to carry. Pack the supplies tightly. Water should not be able to get inside.

3 Do not overpack. Only necessary items should go in the kit. Too many items can make the kit too heavy. Finding things quickly could be difficult.

4 The best way to know if a disaster kit works well is to test it. Try taking the kit on a camping trip. See if everything needed is inside. If something important is missing, be sure to add it.

What You Need
- sterile adhesive bandages
- safety pins
- soap
- latex gloves
- sterile gauze pads
- scissors
- tweezers
- moist towelettes
- antiseptic
- thermometer
- ice pack
- flashlight
- extra batteries
- eye wash solution

Key Words

debris: scattered pieces of trash or damaged materials

engineers: people who build machines and structures

fault lines: sections in Earth's surface where tectonic plates collide with each other

myths: stories created by ancient people to explain natural events

oscillation: a steady, rhythmic movement of an object for a period of time

seismic: relating to earthquakes or Earth's crust

seismic activity: the frequency, amount, and strength of earthquakes in an area during a period of time

seismograph: a device that measures the strength of seismic activity within Earth

seismologists: scientists that study activity in the layers within Earth

Titans: a family of giants in Greek mythology that ruled Earth before the traditional Greek gods came to power

tremors: vibrations in Earth's crust

trident: a three pronged spear used as a fishing tool and military weapon

United States Geological Survey (USGS): a scientific branch of the United States government that studies the landscape of the country, including the possibility and detection of earthquakes

vertical: upright or going up or down

Index

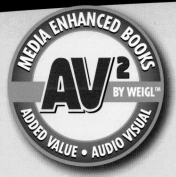

Log on to www.av2books.com

AV² by Weigl brings you media enhanced books that support active learning. Go to www.av2books.com, and enter the special code found on page 2 of this book. You will gain access to enriched and enhanced content that supplements and complements this book. Content includes video, audio, weblinks, quizzes, a slide show, and activities.

AV² Online Navigation

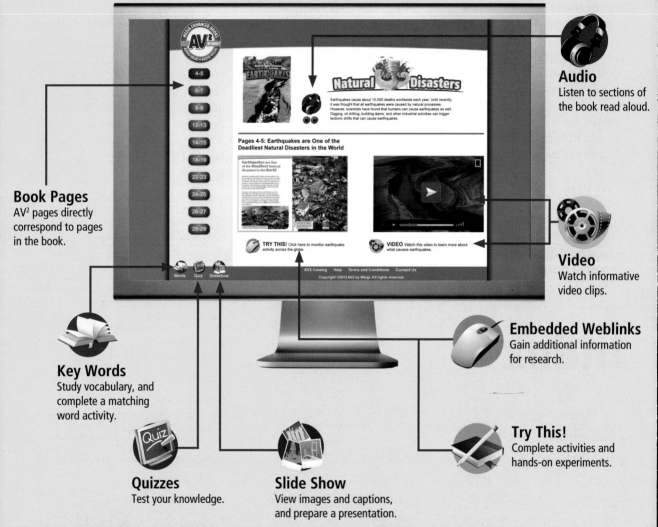

Audio
Listen to sections of the book read aloud.

Book Pages
AV² pages directly correspond to pages in the book.

Video
Watch informative video clips.

Key Words
Study vocabulary, and complete a matching word activity.

Embedded Weblinks
Gain additional information for research.

Try This!
Complete activities and hands-on experiments.

Quizzes
Test your knowledge.

Slide Show
View images and captions, and prepare a presentation.

AV² was built to bridge the gap between print and digital. We encourage you to tell us what you like and what you want to see in the future.

Sign up to be an AV² Ambassador at www.av2books.com/ambassador.